HOPE FOR THE NIGHT SEASON

HOPE FOR THE NIGHT SEASON

The Darkest Hour Before Dawn

ELAINE WHITE

authorHOUSE®

AuthorHouse™
1663 Liberty Drive
Bloomington, IN 47403
www.authorhouse.com
Phone: 1-800-839-8640

© 2014 Elaine White. All rights reserved.

*No part of this book may be reproduced, stored in
a retrieval system, or transmitted by any means
without the written permission of the author.*

Published by AuthorHouse   10/24/2014

ISBN: 978-1-4969-4694-2 (sc)

*Any people depicted in stock imagery provided by Thinkstock are models,
and such images are being used for illustrative purposes only.
Certain stock imagery © Thinkstock.*

This book is printed on acid-free paper.

*Because of the dynamic nature of the Internet, any web addresses or
links contained in this book may have changed since publication and
may no longer be valid. The views expressed in this work are solely those
of the author and do not necessarily reflect the views of the publisher,
and the publisher hereby disclaims any responsibility for them.*

*Scripture quotations marked KJV are from the Holy Bible, King James
Version (Authorized Version). First published in 1611. Quoted from the KJV
Classic Reference Bible, Copyright © 1983 by The Zondervan Corporation*

About the Author

If you ask her what her motivation is, she will tell you, **Jesus is her passion and praise is her purpose**. Elaine is a worshiper on fire for the Lord. She loves the Lord and makes declaration that God is her life. Her vision is to become a worldwide ministry inspiring and encouraging people everywhere to find God. This awesome woman of God ministers the word of God through her poetic writings of exhortation and encouragement. She wants everyone to know there is always **HOPE** regardless of the situation and circumstances in your daily life. Her motto is, "any day with God is better than one without him." She believes in the soon return of Jesus Christ and wants to admonish everyone to be ready. She has a quiet and meek spirit but yet she proclaims the powerful word of God under the leading and direction of the Holy Spirit with boldness and courage.

Faith Inspired Seeds of Hope (FISH) ministry was birth in 2006. She considers it an honor and privilege to fulfill her assignment as a fisher of men. Elaine has authored two books, *Faith Inspired Seeds of Hope and Garden of Hope*.

Elaine is an ordained minister and lives with husband, Elder Ron in Muncie, IN. They are active ministers who serve under the anointed leadership of Dr. Kevin Woodgett, at The Church of the Living God, Muncie, IN. Together they share this vision and mission for Christ.

Contents

About the Author v
Special Acknowledgements.. ix
Dedication xi
Introduction... xiii
God... 1
Holy Ground 4
Seasons... 5
Now Faith 7
The Promise 8
Opposition 10
Perfection 12
Kiss On My Face...14
Called 16
Count It All Joy 18
False Face...19
Seek Him 21
You Are My Shepherd 22
Let Me See You 23
Midnight... 24
My Weakness.. 26
Hanging On 27
Forgive to Live 28
Midst of the Fire 29
You Know Lord... 30
A Different Place..31
The Passion of Christ 32
Pushed 33
Let Me Be 35
Your Word 37
Unsung Heroes 39

Sin	41
Be Still	43
Live to Die	45
The Journey	47
Beware	48
Your Will Be Done	50
Chastening	51
Quiet	52
Darkness	54
Midnight Season	55
Sing in the Dark	56
Front Line	57
Not What It Seems	58
Reverse	59
Fresh	60
Believe	61
Possess the Promise	64
Listen For My Will	66
Awake Saints!	68
Return of Christ	69
Spiritual War	70
Last Days	72
The Remnant	74
Jesus is the Light	75
House of Clay	76
Deliver Me	77
Prayer Changes Things	79
He Knows	80
Testimony	81
I Can't Afford	83
There Will Be Glory	85
Good Morning	87

Special Acknowledgements

I give all thanks, praise, glory and honor to My Lord and Savior, Jesus Christ. I am so blessed to have been chosen to be one of His. Without the leading of the Holy Spirit nothing I do would be possible. As a willing vessel, it is my desire to use all my gifts as ministry to bring Him glory and to reach souls for the Kingdom of God.

I praise God for the prayers and support of my natural and spiritual family members. I love you and may God continue to bless you all!

I want to appreciate a very special young lady who has been an awesome blessing to our ministry. She has truly been a God-sent, my sister, armor-bearer, confidante, prayer partner and loyal friend, Danielle Denton-Johnson. Grace and peace be unto you and may God continue to use you mightily for the Kingdom. I love you.

And last be not least, my number one supporter, best friend, wonderful husband and life partner Elder Ron E. White; continue to let the Lord use you mighty man of valor. I love you!

Dedication

To my parents, Elder Henry Sr. and Edna Clayton

Daddy has been the patriarch of our family and I am thankful for his guidance and faithfulness. He has exhibited an inner strength that has endured throughout the seasons of life. Never once have I heard him complain, but rather he remained constant and steadfast in his love and obedience to Christ.

Mama has been the matriarch, the quiet strength of our family. Her love is unending and she is one you can depend upon. She has been a beacon of light to this family; her continual prayers have seen this family through every season. She has a mother's love that is unmatched and she is a true woman of God.

I thank you both for being the glue that has held our family together. You taught us how to pray and how to have a true relationship with the Heavenly Father. I want to say, "Thank you" for being very fine parents and examples of the love of Christ.

Dad and Mom, I love you!

Introduction

Weeping may endure for **only** one night, but the morning light will bring forth joy! Your night may seem like a lifetime, but it is only for a season. Remember it is the darkest just before the dawn. The word of God tells us in James 1:2 "Count it all joy when you meet trials of various kinds, for you know that the testing of your faith produces steadfastness." We are to count it a blessing while we are being tested. As Christians, we may think the writer James was being somewhat unreasonable by what he was saying, but in reality, the trials are working in our favor, for our good. God is working our perfection. They are blessings in disguise. James 1:12, states, "Blessed is the man who remains steadfast under trial, for when he has stood the test he will receive the crown of life."

Christians, be of good courage, think it not strange because the Bible declares that those who live godly shall suffer persecution. As written in John 15:2, this is the pruning process, "Every branch in me that does not bear fruit he takes away, and every branch that does bear fruit he prunes, that it may bear more fruit." This process is necessary for the growth of each believer.

Elaine White

This process has many names, some may call it the testing of your faith, the Job experience, the refining process, the purification process, the chastening of God, but I call it

…the night season.

God

My Father
Is perfect in all His ways
At His command the wind and waves obey
Endless
Timeless
No boundaries, no limits
He exceeds all
Everything submits to His call
His thoughts are not like mine
He exist in and out of time
He is All knowing, All powerful
Ever present
He is wonderful
Before the beginning and the end
From everlasting to everlasting
His Word will stand
He supersedes our knowledge and our understanding
He is God, He is a Spirit
Supernatural being
He is Ruler over the earth
King of everything
Creator of the universe
Forever He will reign

He sits high in the heavens and
Looks low to where I am
He is Judah's Lion and
Yet was humble as a lamb
Holy and righteous, faithful and true
He does just what He promises to do
He was, is and is to come
Past, present and who is yet to come
Worthy and Supreme
Royalty at best
Only He can assure eternal rest
To know God is eternal life
He gives us breath through His living Word
He is the Bread of Life
He is my Father and He is my God
From beginning to the end
He was, is and has already been
He is Alpha and Omega
The first and the last
He does what He wants
He does not have to ask
He is ever present
He has no origin
Darkness and void flees from His face

His presence lights up whatever He embrace
He is not afraid
He is aware of where we are
He let us know He is near
He is never too far
His presence provides us insight
Gives us strength to fight
He fills all time and space
Showers us with love and grace
Before there was a what or where, why or when
His thoughts were where it all begin, creation and man
God is God and beside Him there is none other.

Holy Ground

Bow down
Worship the King
He is Master of everything
Let his praises ring
Behold his awesomeness
His wonderful greatness
In his presence is full joy
His riches are more than any human can afford
He is calling for his people to stand
On holy ground
Spread the "good news" until
The trumpet sounds
He wants our submission and attention
Not to mention
He wants us to know when
We enter into his presence
We are on holy ground
Bow down and worship the King.

Seasons

To everything there is a time and season
Often they may come without warning
But there is always a reason
A season of unrest, battling the fierce test
Reassuring yourself that God knows best
Like a whirlwind, taking your breath away
Wondering what will confront you today
Midlife crisis, economy woes
Breakdown within the family
And on and on it goes
A season of favor, rest and peace
Wars and battles now have cease
Abundance and overflow all around you
Everything you touch and everything you do
Is blessed
Seasons come and seasons go
We must be ready to go with the flow
Seasons come to bring a change
Many times things are rearranged

You may find yourself in a place of
Uncertainty, the unfamiliar and unknown
It has purpose and plans for you to grow
Seasons like spring, summer, winter and fall
Will surely one day touch us all
Thankfully winter last only for a while
We must endure whatever God allows
Spring is new birth, renewal and life
Time to forgive and get things right
Summer is a time to enjoy the blessings from above
To spread the gospel and share God's love
Fall is harvest time when things are ripe and ready
Make sure your steps are ordered and steady
Winter is cold and the light is growing dim
Be aware that we must keep our lamps trim
And burning bright
Let Christ be our light to keep our feet right
As we journey through the seasons of life.

Now Faith

The **just** live by their faith, the **now faith**
The faith to believe and take God at His word
No matter how crazy or absurd
Faith works by acting upon the Word of God
Mountains move because of **now faith**
Doors open because of **now faith**
Healing and deliverance takes place because of **now faith**
We must possess this **now faith** to make it day by day
For God said it is the only way
Without faith it is impossible to please the Lord
Lacking faith is something we cannot afford
We must obtain it to do God's will
We must believe in it and be Holy filled
Faith is not seeing before you will believe
But believing before you can see or receive
Faith is essential for every believer
For when you have **now faith,** you will then become a receiver of the promises of God.
FAITH IS NOW.

The Promise

The promise is not the riches of this land
It is not fortune or fame
It is not for unbelievers but
Those who wear his name
God promised us a land flowing with milk and honey
He did not mean by the world's standards of high position or money
But He promised that we would have all that we need
Bountiful riches and treasures indeed
He promised us peace within our land
He promise us wealth beyond what we could understand
Safety and protection would be ours too
He promise to always see us through
Treasures like mercy and grace that one cannot buy
His faithfulness every morning and favor on our side
Wisdom and knowledge with every step we take
Guiding our decisions so we will not make mistakes

The promise of reigning and ruling in this place
Taking authority over the enemy and controlling our space
Walking and speaking the Word and believing into being
Calling those things that are not even when you are not seeing
Riches like possessing and operating within the anointing of the Holy Spirit
Which is given to those who believe, it is not earned by our own merit
Promises of living in the abundance of overflow
Really, who would not want to go
The promise is for all who would believe, for every generation
God promised his blessings would flow to every nation
Whatever God has promised you, you should **believe it**, because it will surely come to pass
Are you ready to step into your promise?

Opposition

Opposition comes to build character
Inner strength and self discipline
A wise man once said, "You cannot produce in conduct what you have not produced in character"*
Character is maintained in the midst of the fire
Integrity is upheld and although you may get tired
Opposition makes you uncomfortable and pushes you beyond your comfort zone
It strengthens you to withstand even when you must stand alone
Opposition is allowed to come into our lives to prove our faith
Opposition put you in position for God to be glorified
It is for our cleansing, sanctification, as we are purified
Opposition does not feel good; it causes the flesh to die as it should
As the Bible tells us, we must not think it strange when fiery trials come because there must be a testing of our faith
It is the path we all must take and
It is okay when I don't understand

It is okay that I don't know the details of His plan
It is okay when I can't see my way
It's okay when I don't have the words to say
It is okay because He is teaching me to trust and have faith
It is okay because I must follow what He said
It is okay when I want to ask why
It is okay when sometimes all I want to do is cry
It is okay, I know everything will be alright
It is okay because it will only be midnight for one night
God, I know you are the Master and Creator of all things
You are in control all the time no matter how crazy it may seem
Every road block, every ditch or valley comes to make me strong
I am just not sure how good can come out of so much wrong
But you know, you are always aware, nothing catches you off guard
You are God, Wonderful and Awesome, Ruler and Lord that is who you are and although opposition comes I am okay.
* Quote from Dr. Kevin Woodgett, sermon on "Character"

Perfection

He is perfecting me beyond
My belief
Beyond what I can see
Molding me into
His image and likeness
He is perfecting me
I must believe
It is all working for my good
Producing in me all that should
Be in my life
Fruit of righteousness
Holiness and truth
Peace and love
With many promises too
He is perfecting me
Through the fire so
I will die out to my desire, so
When the enemy comes in like a flood

He covers me with His own blood
He is perfecting me
Until He can see
His attributes within my heart
He knew from the start
I want to enter into the pearly gates
So I will endure whatever it takes
He is perfecting me to see clearly
In the spirit
Taking authority over evil
He is giving me grace to bear it
He is perfecting his love in me
Teaching me to give so I will receive
An abundance of blessings and overflow
So I can go
Into the promise land
He is perfecting me.

Kiss On My Face

I woke up this morning with your kiss on my face
You let me know you were all in my space
To erase all my doubts and calm my fear
To carry my burdens and wipe every tear
You ordained and prepared my day for me
To protect and keep me from what I cannot see
All I will need for today has already been provided
Just follow your steps and I will not be misguided
You let me know there was nothing to fear
With every step I take, you would be near
Covering me from harm's way
And at the right time, you'll give me what to say
You have already assigned angels to fight for me
In the realm in which this world does not believe
The spiritual realm really does exist
This world believes it is just a myth
Thank you Lord for your reassurance and
Renewed strength to help me maintain endurance
I am walking in your might not my own
Your amazing power and purpose has been shown
Demonstrated and recognized in my life
I have no resentment, bitterness or strife
I come into agreement with your will
You have told me to be silent and stand still
Your awesome power will be revealed
The world will soon know who I call
My Savior, Master, Lord and King

You are the only reason I continue to sing
You really do love and care for your own
You are my heavenly father who sits on the throne
Beholding the evil and the good
Rendering mercy to all who should receive judgment
You know what is best and I must pass each test
Your fire will purify my inner soul
The water will cleanse and make me whole
Thank you for providing my armor and shield
Teaching me how to walk as I yield
Myself totally to be used by you
I crucify this flesh so you can do
Whatever you want with me
As I release my faith to believe
I am the clay within your hand
To be shaped and molded at your command
You know the way you have chosen for me
With your guidance, I will gladly follow thee
Thank you for the "kiss" which lets me know
You are always and forever in control
I trust you Lord, your every word is true
I know you will certainly see me through
What you have started in me will be complete
When at last our faces will meet
Whether through death or in the air
I just want to be ready when you appear
So I can receive more of your kisses.

Called

Called for the cause of Christ
To stand for justice and
Do what is right
Called to be the "light" of this world
Called to let your voice be heard
Cry loud and spare not
We have been called to make a difference
Sin is running rampant throughout the land
Ruining everything good that it can
We must fight against injustice and sin
God has promised us the victory, we will win
Doing "good" does not always feel good
Sometimes we must suffer for doing what is right
God has given us the weapons we need to fight
We must keep HIS focus in sight
And let Christ be our light
Every believer has been called to work
It does not matter if the world treats us like dirt
Still we must condemn prejudice and wrong

Despite the fact, it has been accepted for so long
We cannot be fearful or weak, although
It is a blessing to be meek
God has not given us the spirit of fear but
Power and authority because He is near
He dwells inside within our heart
He knows the enemy desires to tear us apart
We must come against
Ungodly standards and immoral ways
We must not let the world sway
Our beliefs, values or our truths
We must be a witness to the lost and dying
Not allowing the enemy to keep lying, but
To tell them Christ is their true hope
He is life's **only** antidote
Called to be a beacon of light in this dark world that is decaying day by day
Every day letting us know He is on His way
Will you answer the call?

Count It All Joy

Count it all joy, when it is painful to bear
God has chosen you; He knows your every care
Rejoice that you were hand-picked for the test
Endure the refining process to secure your eternal rest
No it does not feel good to our flesh but
The Lord knows what is best
He has ordered our steps and the road we must take
We must be willing vessels for Him to mold and make
Us into His image, and
To be without spot or blemish, so
We may enter in around the throne
Counting it all joy because we are not alone
Count it all joy even though it may hurt
Keep trusting God even when you are treated like dirt
For Christ will soon have the last say, he will avenge his children when He comes to take them away
You were designed to survive; it is the flesh that must die
Die to sin, so the inner man might be strengthen with power from on high, count it all joy!

False Face

Hiding behind the false face
While inside you ache and ache
Trying hard not to break
But you know you are a fake
You have wore this false face for so long
The pretense has convinced you it's not wrong
You reason within yourself
"This is me."
You tell yourself, "This is the way it has to be
How can I let others see
Who I really am"
So you pretend that everything is alright
Acting as though you cannot see the Light
The Light that comes to shine so bright
On your pathway to guide you right
Right into His presence and His care

He knows all and is everywhere
You may not be aware; you are naked in His sight
He is Alpha and Omega and He has hindsight
Let Him heal your brokenness and pain
He will remove all your guilt and shame
Invite Him in by calling on His name
No longer will you have to hide
You can live free and abide
In His everlasting love and grace
With peace in your heart and on your face
Get rid of the false and put on the real
Jesus' love is what you will feel
When you ask Him into your heart
He will renew you as you start
Trusting and obeying His commands
Doing all that you can
To let His light shine through you
No longer hiding behind the false face
Living a lie that is so fake but
Now you can walk in God's love and grace.

Seek Him

We must first seek His face
He will show us His loving grace
He will fill us with power and authority
He said we can resist the enemy and He will flee
We must seek His divine will
It is His desire for us to be Holy-filled
When we seek His face, the way gets brighter
He will give us directions and make our burdens lighter
Lord, we seek your face not your hand
For we truly understand
This is the path to your righteousness
And you will reveal your holiness as
We seek your face
Wise men still seek Him.

You Are My Shepherd

Lord, you are my shepherd, I am the sheep
I will follow you regardless of how much I weep
Like a good father you care for me
You shelter me from harm and dangers I cannot see
I rest within your embrace
All my needs are met
You are my strong tower and my safety net
You lead me down paths I may not want to go
I realize it is for your glory because you love me so
You see the best in me that no one else can
You know the plans you have for me
though I may not understand
You are my shepherd I know your voice
I am so glad I made you my choice
Goodness and mercy shall follow me
Your truth and love will be the light that I see
I am glad you are my shepherd and I shall not want.

Let Me See You

Lord, I want to see only you
When I am going thru
Not the circumstances I am in
But focused on you, guarantees
I will win
I want you to get all the glory
As I write this story
Because it all belongs to you
No matter what things may look like
Still to you, praise is due
Regardless the difficulty or severity of the test
I must trust and believe
You know best
It may be dark in my life at this time
I know the victory will soon be mine
Let me see only you.

Midnight

At the edge about to go over
Feeling the weight of the world on my shoulder
Who or what will rescue me
Who or what can set my free
Pressure on the left and on the right
Seeming no relief in sight
But
I am a Christian, how can this be
How are these issues swallowing me
I tithe and pray and go to church
I read God's word yet still I hurt
Everywhere I turn there is trouble
I pray to God to deliver me on the double
Woe is me, my flesh begins to say
Making me doubtful and afraid
Sometimes I feel so alone
Where is God to console
Fighting wars without and within
Fighting my mind so my flesh will not sin
O wretched soul of mine
I know God said I will be fine
I got to believe God has a reason
I will find strength, because it is only for a season
It is midnight, dark as night
All hell is breaking loose right before the sunlight
This midnight can only stay for one night
Then my God will step in and make all things right
Let satan shoot his best shot
I will not give in, I just will not

I may be weak and hanging by a string
But **Christ is my help**, **my every thing**
Yes, I may be at the edge but His hand is holding me
He will not let me go over, he's my security
Midnight is an appointed time and season
With specific purpose and reason
It comes unwelcomed to build our faith
It is not pleasant and yes it does ache
Be of good cheer during the midnight
If you look real close you will see the **Light**.

My Weakness

When I am weak, then are you strong
According to your Word, not because of any wrong
It is because of your kindness and steadfast love
Your mercy and grace poured on me from above
The test and trials causes my flesh to submit
I am not successful just from intelligence or wit
I must learn to surrender to your perfect will
Be willing to endure and swallow the bitter pill
If you live godly you will suffer for Christ
Jesus was our example, He was the perfect sacrifice
My weakness let me know who is really in control
It also makes me aware that satan is after my soul
I must decrease so you can increase and be seen in me
I want you to get the glory; the only way it must be
In my weakness producing meekness
You reveal yourself to me
Telling me to yield to your authority
When I am weak then you are strong.

Hanging On

I am hanging on your promises
I am clinging to your word
I do not know another way
So I just listen for your voice
Your voice is what comforts me
It protects me from all harm
It warns me of the enemy by sounding the alarm
Where can I go and to whom do I seek
You are the only one I depend on when
I am weary and weak
I may be hanging barely by a thin thread
Still I rely on you for my daily bread
As I read and meditate I am fed
All your promises are true
So I look for you to come through
I have **HOPE** as I hang on.

Forgive to Live

I want to forgive so I can live the life promised to me
The life God wants for me when I believe
I believe God's word is true
I must do what He says to do
In order to receive the promises He has for me
I must let my faith be my eyes to see
He really knows just what I need
I must let His word be the seed to grow me
into maturity as I walk into my destiny
I want to forgive so I can live the abundant life
Free of resentment, bitterness or strife
I desire everything God has for me
I want his forgiveness, grace, faithfulness, and mercy
I want to forgive because
It is the only way I can live
I must forgive just like my Father up above
He decided to love His enemies to
show the world He is love.
Today, because I am forgiven, I forgive.

Midst of the Fire

In the midst of the fire
Trust God to lift you higher
High above your circumstance
Go ahead, do your victory dance
The fire is not to destroy you
But to purify you through and through
It is to draw you close to Him
To take you into another realm
It builds your character as you deny yourself
It is to burn all your fleshy desires until there is none left
It strengthens your integrity and makes you strong
It help you to do right when your flesh want to do wrong
It will establish your stance to stand with confidence and conviction
To endure each test and be committed during transition
In the midst of the fire, you must not grow tired because in due season you will reap if you faint not.

You Know Lord

Lord, you know that I am not strong
Yet you told me to stand against wrong
Although, I am not sure how long
You will have me endure before you change my song
You are my strength when I am weak
Your will and desire are what I seek
I am not perfect and sometimes not meek
Sometimes all I want to do is weep
My outward appearance may seem to be strong
But on the inside, oh how I long to be home
In your embrace, sheltered from all this wrong
With no more worries, no more cares
No more pressures, no more tears
Then I remember your word to strengthen my heart
I must let it become a part
Of every step that I take
No matter how hard my heart may ache
I know that you care for me
Thank you for loving me tenderly.

A Different Place

I am in a different place
A place of mercy and grace where all around me
I see God's face
A place of truth and reality
Although things may not
Appear what they ought to be
A place of wealth and peace
Where the internal wars have cease
A place where God's spirit dwells
As He speaks and declares to me
"All is well"
A place of love and hope
Where the view is from the
Spiritual scope
A different place
A good place to be
Filled with God's love and favor
Just for me.

The Passion of Christ

I see God and His glory in the earth
I believe in His virgin birth
He died so I could know my worth
Everlasting life was finally brought forth
The passion of Christ—to give His life
He gave the ultimate sacrifice
This was love
Why did He love humanity
He gave His all so we could be free
It was God's purpose and plan
That Christ would redeemed the sinner man
Back to Himself
It was His will
In obedience He did fulfill
His destiny
Now it is up to you and me
To receive what was done for us indeed
He bore the beatings, suffered and endured the shame
Soon, He will return for those who wear His name.

Pushed

You have been pushed for purpose
Pushed
Never to return to the place where you have been
Once in your life
Pushed
Out of your comfort zone unto the unfamiliar
The unknown
Pushed
To be different, to do God's will
Changed and anointed
To go forth into what God has called you to
Pushed
Out of your mindset and ideas so HE will fill
You with His desires and His purpose
Pushed
Into your destiny and your ministry
Your later will be greater than your past
Pushed

To be stronger and wiser
Pushed
Unto maturity, growing in Christ
Pushed
Into some tight places
Many times I could not see nor
Understand
Pushed
To forgive so I can live
The life God has called me to
Pushed
Crucifying this flesh for His name sake
Suffering through pain and shame
Pushed for purpose
For God knows the plans He has for me
Learning to trust and just believe
Pushed
To say "Yes Lord" to whatever He says.

Let Me Be

Rest in me
Let it be
I see farther than
You can see
I know best
Trust me and rest
I will see you through this test
Take a breath
Ease your step
I will make the way
While you relax
My yoke is easy
My burdens light
I will give faith for your eyesight
I will right the wrong
I will keep you strong
When you rely on me

Lose your grip and
Let me be
Let me be your strong tower
To run to when you need power
Let me be your strength
When you are weak and bent
Let me be your guide
With me your feet will not slide
Let me be your joy in sorrow
I will be your hope for tomorrow
Cast your cares on me
Trust me and believe
I will be your way
When there seems to be no way
Let me be
I will make everything
Okay.

Your Word

Your Word is full of love and grace
As I read your word, you reveal your face
Your Word is powerful and strong
Obeying it will keep me from going wrong
Your Word is the way the truth and light
It will guide me in the path that is right
It is a comforter when I am sad
It lifts my spirit and makes me glad
It encourages me when my days are dark
It makes me happy, I will sing like a lark
Your Word is faithful and true
Every promise you make, you come through
The Word of God is alive and it is real
It is not just a book but something I can feel
Your Word is life, the very essence of my being
It gives me hope and a reason for living
I know I have your word but sometimes I wonder
How long must the innocent suffer and be wronged
What will it take and why does it seem so long

In your Word, you promised to fight on my behalf
You promised to whip the enemy so I could laugh
Laugh because I am an over comer with the victory
You can do more than I can, if I just believe
I know the innocent are covered in your care
I know you have the all Seeing Eye that is everywhere
I know you know why and you know when
You knew from the beginning how this will all end
In your own timing when you deemed best
I know this is about growing my faith, because it is only a test
You know all the details and you know the way
You know every circumstance and just what to say
Help my faith to remind me constantly throughout this fight
Help me to see your bright light even through this night
Help me to endure the fire maintaining my integrity
As you purify and mold me into what you desire for me.
I am thankful for your word.

Unsung Heroes

God knows their toils and pain
Heart aches, hurt and shame
Yet they remain faithful just the same
It doesn't matter that no one
Knows their name because
They work for the King,
Not to be seen
They know their purpose and
What life really means
They stand for justice, what is good and right
They are willing vessels to be God's light
In this dark world, cold and cruel
They cry out loud that Christ still rules
They stand in the midst of opposition
Letting the enemy know their position
With Christ on their side, they cannot lose
He uses whomever he choose
Unsung heroes, thankful God knows who they are
They are all over the world, both near and far.

Sin

Bound by sin, seemingly no end
Look as though there is no way to win
Where and when did you begin
Drowning in this whirlpool of sin
Wondering now
How did you get here and when will it all end
Well
Disobedience got you into this fine mess
Unfortunately
You did not realize you were already blessed
Rather
You enjoyed the pleasures of sin for a season
Not realizing there was a cost, this is the reason
Chains of darkness and strong bondages hold you tight
As you try searching for the true "Light"
Thru the grimness and evils of the night
Reaching for a hand
Someone to understand and to pull
you from your sinking sand
Sin is not a friend
It only wants to reel you in
As it feeds you lies and deceit
Making promises it can't meet
Only to find out in the end
That eternal damnation is what you will win
Sin will leave you empty and void
Of the things you once enjoyed
It will rob you of joy and peace and

You will wish all the madness to cease
It will cost you more than you ever wanted to pay
And will not let you easily just walk away
It will steal and destroy your mind
True happiness you will never find
It will lead you far away from home and will
Isolate you and make you feel all alone
Sin is an enemy of your soul
The devil fighting for control
This war begun long ago
In the Garden of Eden where Adam first sinned
And this is where the story begins
But sin can be conquered; this is
why Christ died on the cross
To redeemed mankind back from being lost
If you really understood
The battle has been won, victory is sure
Forsake the sinful life and let righteousness endure
Evil shall be conquered and destroyed by all good
God has promised the believers certainly it would
This war of sin is not of flesh and blood
It is spiritual
Sin is over ruled when you fight
Trust in God and obey doing what is right
He will give you weapons, godly wisdom and insight
To defeat the enemy
If you just believe.

Be Still

Be still, don't move
Let me take care of you
Only I have the wisdom
To bring you through
I am Alpha and Omega
The Beginning and the End
I am the only one who can
Guarantee you will win
You can't see the way, you must believe
You must use your faith for eyes to see
I want to take care of you
But you must trust me to do what I do
I have the best plan
I know what road to choose
Obey my word and you will not lose
Be still and know that I am your God
Don't be distracted by what you see
Trust my word and just believe
The enemy has no power over you
I allow the tests that you go through
All power is within my hand
Know who you are and understand
You are just passing through down here; this world is not your home
Keep focus on the path you are on for you are not alone
Distractions comes in all shapes and forms to get you off course

Keep your eyes on me, let me be the force
To lead and guide you with each step that you take
Hold on to my hand, seek me first for every choice you make
I will give you the strength you need to endure thru each day
Just acknowledge me in all your ways and don't forget to pray
Distractions come to cloudy your view
To make you feel you don't know what to do
They come to cause doubt, worry and fear
Know that I am very near
Nothing takes me by surprise nor unaware
Cast your cares on me and your burdens I will bear
No weapon that the enemy forms against you will succeed
Study and meditate upon my word and you will see
How I stopped the mouths of lions and took fire out of the flame
I fed five thousand with five fish and healed those who called on my name
I am Alpha and Omega, the beginning and the end
I knew before the foundation of the world, when time would begin
I am strong and mighty, no one can pluck you out of my hand
I am the reason the world exist, child, now do you understand
When you put your trust in me, you cannot lost
So when distractions come to you, you must choose
Not to move, just
Be still and know that I am God.

Live to Die

Many do not understand why
As a direct result of man's sin
Our life on this earth is brief
And must come to an end
Death is so final in our mind
That is why Christ came to earth, lived and died
To redeem mankind and to offer eternal life
To all who would believe
He took the sting out of death when He went to hell
After three days He ascended to tell
The good news that we do not have to fear
If we die in Him, we are only asleep
Although our physical bodies will decease
If you want your spirit man to live in peace
You must die daily to sin in this flesh
So you can live eternally and have sweet rest
When you have a true relationship with the Father above
You should look with anticipation, truth and love
Because to be absent from this body

Is to be present with our Lord
Where peace, joy and happiness dwell
Where living is great and all is well
No more sorrow or no more pain
His presence will be the light and no more rain
We are not on this earth to stay
Thank God, He has already provided a way
For us to escape the fire and destruction coming soon
That will be the unbelievers' imminent doom
We die to live and live to die
Awaiting His return in the twinkling of an eye
That is why it's ok for us to die
We know we will live again on the glory side
Have your house in order and your lamps burning bright
Take the time to right the wrongs so your heart will be right
We never know when God will call back his breath
Just make sure you are in right relationship with the Father
and your reward will be peace and rest.

The Journey

The Lord said to me, take my hand
I said Lord, but I do not understand, I cannot see
He said, I know my child, only believe
Let me lead the way and fill your mouth with what to say
Let me be your guiding light, trust me to give you wisdom and insight
He said, this is why I am here, I am concern with your every care
I will make your pathway clear because I am God and very aware of everything that concerns you
Cast all your cares on the altar because I know what to do
So I did
I gave him my hand and asked him to lead the way, to steady my feet and strengthen me as I pray
He took my hand in His and held it tight
He promised to get me through this terrible night
He promised me eternal life if I would follow him and let Him fight
I said, I trust you Lord on this journey, lead me.

Beware

The devil's ploy is to destroy you
He doesn't care what or who he use
He prefer those closest to your heart
To rip and tear you apart
He utilizes "legitimate" things to pull at your heart strings
He is skillful and canny at this sort of thing
He distracts your focus and obscures your view
He wants you to give up and declare you are through
He is crafty and clever, the master of disguise
He wants to fill your head with his dreadful lies
He wants to destroy you because you are one of God's saints
You are heaven bounded, someplace he ain't
He set up roadblocks to detour your way
You are his target he studies everyday
To knock you off course so you will not pray, and
You will speak negative things you should not say
He knows what appeals to you and how to inflict pain
He wants you to deny your God and worship his name
But He can't do any more than what our God allows

His time on earth is temporary, he can only continue for a short while
Our Lord and Savior will destroy him when He comes back for His bride
Satan, his imps and followers will be condemned to hell for their sins, lies and pride
Be encouraged and strengthen, continue to fast and pray
This is the way to defeat the enemy as the Bible says
You do not have to be wearied when doing well
Just beware he is trying to take your soul to hell
Stay focus on the straight and narrow way
Until God comes for you whether in the sky or the grave
Beware, watch and pray.

Your Will Be Done

Your will be done, you are the one
Who knows what is best
And when to speak rest
To my worried soul
For only you can console me
At my time of need
I will listen and take heed
To your word that I hear as
You whisper in my ear
Telling me that you are near and not to fear
Your will be done, you are the one
To lead me when I cannot see
You are my guiding light
Giving me sight in my darkest night
Teaching how to be still and let you fight
For the battle is not mine
And every time
I can claim the victory
Your will Lord, be done.

Chastening

Son, despise not the chastening of the Lord
It is to cleanse you and make you whole
After all, He is the potter and you are the clay
He wants you to yield your will, trust and obey
So He can have His way in you
To produce a product that He can use
Do not rebel or run from His hand
He knows what to do and how much you can stand
There is no pleasure in His chastening
But He is making you into a new "being"
Perfected by His hand at His discretion
Not to wander in your own direction
Without Him you do not know what way to take
On your own, you will make costly mistakes
Yield to the Lord, let Him have His way
To discipline and direct you until you hear Him say
"This is my child in whom I am well pleased!"

Quiet

Quiet my soul, take a rest
God is in control
He knows what is best
The storms all around
Are only test
To strengthen my faith so I can last
When all around looks like sinking sand
I must remember the God who
Holds my hand
The battle is not given to the swift
Nor the strong
But to those who endure, to those who
Hang on
I got this assurance
God will fight on my behalf
Let the enemy go ahead
I will have the last laugh

I must stay encouraged to finish this task
Stay focus and prayerful
Believing He will do what I ask
I know God has a purpose and a plan
It is not for me to know or understand
It is not what it looks like
This I must believe
I am not looking with my natural but
Spiritual eyes to see
Quiet soul, as I listen for His voice
When Jesus speaks
Everything must stand still at His command
Even the wind and waves understand
Only He can speak peace and calm the storm
He speaks peace
To my troubled mind
Only He can give me
What I could not find
Quiet soul, rest indeed
I am sure He knows what is best for me.

Darkness

Black dark
No light in sight
Panic fills the room
Madness, despair and gloom
Then---in the darkness
Jesus, the Master speaks
Peace be still
Everything stands attention to His will
Commanding the darkness to dispel
Letting me know all is well
The blackness around now turns into light
He brightens my path and gives me sight
I know now everything is alright
I can see the daylight.

Midnight Season

Midnight is a season with a definite reason
It brings about change
And can rearrange your life
It is not at all as it appears
However it usually produces fear
The absence of light…is darkness
Night and day are both the same
To our Father
He is not bothered
Nor is He taken by surprise
It comes to crucify our flesh
So Christ may arise
No one likes the midnight
It is difficult to see the light
But
God does His best work
During the midnight hour
When all hope seems lost
He shows up and reveals His power.

Sing in the Dark

Sing in the dark
When you can't see through the storm
Sing in the dark
He promised to keep you safe and warm
Sing in the dark
When you can't feel no one is there
Sing in the dark
Because His presence is near
Sing in the dark
He promised to be your guide
Sing in the dark
Under His wings you can hide
Sing in the dark
Like a lark chirping on a fresh morn
because Christ was born
Sing in the dark
For it soon will pass, the morning will
break forth and joy will arrive at last.

Front Line

I am on the front line
Getting hit left and right
I know my change is coming
If I endure this fight
Sometimes feeling bombarded and
wanting to throw in the towel
I must still believe help is coming, even
though I do not know when or how
On the front line
Feels like I am about to lose my mind
Overwhelmed by life's cares and woes
No time for pity, sometimes this is just the way it goes
Trying to maintain, as the attacks become severe
Keeping my composure praying relief will appear
On the front line
Sometimes, not seeing an end in sight, but
I know God has promised, I will win this fight
All around is darkness and night, still
I will look to the Light.

Not What It Seems

It is not at all what it may seem
Feels like a bad dream
Satan is telling me
He has won
Trying to make me feel like I am done
But my God is here with me in the midst of it all
Protecting and fighting so I will not fall
The enemy is ranting and raving mad
Wanting to deceive me to believe he is bad
Honestly, he is so sad
My soul is one he thought he had
It is not what it looks like
Trouble all around, dark and dreary,
Tired of fighting, weak and weary
In the heat of the battle God is there
From beginning to end, He is always near
It is not at all what it may seem.

Reverse

It takes the bad to appreciate the good
It takes sickness to appreciate being whole
It takes trouble to appreciate peace
When it seems like you are losing the battle for the sake of Christ, you are winning
To gain the whole world and lose your soul, you will have accomplished nothing
To die in Christ, is to gain
To be absent from this body is to be present with our Lord
Opposition builds and strengthens character
Pain produces purpose
We must
Love our enemies and pray for those who hate us because it brings blessings
It doesn't make sense, but it does make faith*
When our society says we are "entitled" to fight back, we must forgive
We must give, in order to receive
It takes the night to appreciate the **Light**.
*Quote from Dr. Kevin Woodgett

Fresh

Fresh anointing
Presence of God
Fall on me like the morning dew
Renewing my mind and spirit
Fall on me, breathe on me
Give me faith to see
Fresh anointing
Pour into my heart
Your word as I start
A brand new day
Show me your will and your way
Fill me with your Holy Spirit
Give me grace and mercy
So I will know what to do and say
Fall on me, fresh and new
Fall on me like the morning dew
Like fresh manna sent from you
Revive and restore me through and through
Fall fresh on me.

Believe

Suicidal thoughts keep racing thru my head
Telling me it is better to be dead
Then I realize these are lies of the enemy
In the grave is where he wants me to be
I must realize my life is not mine to take
To succumb to these thoughts will be a mistake
For hell will then be my home
I know heaven is where I really belong
I know I am in a difficult place
One of hopelessness and disgrace
Time after time God has shown mercy and grace
He tells me I can make it through this race
But I don't see how and I don't understand
Because of my life choices

Now I feel less than a man
Life is cold and can be cruel
The devil desires my life to rule
I am struck between a rock and a stone
Feeling so low and all alone
Lord you know I am so weak
I can't eat or sleep
Lately all I do is weep
Oh God, I cry please help me out of this state
I want to enter in at your pearly gate
I know you are asking for my life
I know I should say "yes" but-
I am afraid; I don't want to let you down
I know running away is causing you to frown
Lord, I know you want my full attention
You want to take me to new dimensions
I know the call of God is upon me
But like so many others, I still refuse to believe
Like Jonah, I have ran, refusing to yield
When you want me to submit to your will
As a child, I have been taught your
Word and I know that it is true
You have shown me your plans and
told me just what I must do
I have fought and resisted far too long
I am broken and wounded and I want to come home
Like the Father and the prodigal son
With open arms you wait for me
I know in your presence is where I would rather be

In your presence is peace, in your care I am free
I thank you Lord for not giving up on me
Taking me through the difficulties of life
When I could not see
Almost gave up hope
I believed
I do believe
I will always believe in you.

Possess the Promise

Dwelling in the land of
Milk and honey
In a state of peace and rest
Wholeness, serenity and comfort
No worries, no cares
Where
Godly wisdom is revealed
Knowledge and understanding is poured
Into your spirit
Heavy burdens are lifted
Walking in liberty and victory
Not defeated
Dwelling in that secret place
The secret place of the
Most Holy God
A good land that comes from the
hand of our Almighty Father
A good land overflowing with goodness
and kindness, wealth and riches
A land to possess all that is good as
we strive to be all we should

A land filled with God's promises where enemies
are driven out as we dance and shout
This land
God himself cares for
His heart is there
It is where He dwells
Lord, how do I possess this land
I am just not sure I understand
I know it is beyond mortal man
Help me trust you to hold my hand
The land is your mind, body and soul
The place where the enemy wants control
But…
When I learn to submit to your will
Be quiet and stand still
I learn to possess my land
Willing to be molded and shaped at your command
This is the way to the promise land.

Listen For My Will

God says
Listen for my will
Wait until
I give direction
For guidance and protection
My ways are not yours
I will open doors
When you follow my way
Obey what I say
Open your heart to show love
Exemplify me, your Father above
There is nothing too hard for me
Release your faith to believe
The world's weapons are not like mine
I created earth, man and time
I will teach you how to war
Do not be bitter nor keep score
When you are weak, then I am strong

I promised never to leave you alone
When you are sad
I will make you glad by
Renewing the fire you once had
When you are overwhelmed
I will comfort you
I promise never to leave you
Increase your faith enough to believe
If you want to look like me
Your flesh must die
So I can see
ME
My reflection
This is my desire for you
As you submit to
What I ask of you
Stand still and see my salvation
I am the saving grace for all nations!

Awake Saints!

Saints! Awake out of sleep put on strength
Be strong yet so meek
The enemy is prowling as he seek
For the simple, faithless and the weak
He is clever, cunning and deplorable
Deceiving God's children is horrible
If he could, he would deceive the very elect
He is lurking and seeking for the "choice" to select
He knows his time on earth is limited
He wants us to be fearful and very timid
Trying to take those he can to hell, luring them to sin
Saints, please do not give in
This world is corrupt, full of terror and greed
Saints, we must be aware of the need
The need to witness to a dying and lost generation
The need is so great, we must move without hesitation
Saints, we are not here to stay
Soon the trumpet of God will sound
and we will be caught away.
Awake, Saints awake!

Return of Christ

The return of Christ is soon
Any day, night or noon
He is coming for a prepared bride
Those who robes are washed and white
Daily He is taking us through the refining process
Getting rid of all dirt and filthy excess
He is making sure our hearts are clean
Without malice, hatred or any such thing
He is testing our hearts to see if we are real
He knows the truth about how we really feel
He is teaching us this world is not our home
His heavenly abode is where we belong
He is teaching us how to deny this worldly flesh
To bring it under subjection, submit to God and be bless
Yes, Christ return is soon, no man knows the hour though some may presume
Each of us must live as though any day, any hour
We could be rapture by His power, He is coming soon!

Spiritual War

The spiritual world is more real than it may appear
There are spirits, angels and demons everywhere
Warring and fighting- right against wrong
Oppression, depression but some singing the victory song
This realm is so real though it cannot be touch with human hands
With revelation of God's Word and prayers is how we understand
We do not war against flesh and blood nor face or personality
But against devils, demons, and imps, doubt, fear and unbelief
We resist them with the Word of God and they must flee
We fight against evil assignments, plots, plans and perverseness of all kinds
We fight against every evil concept or idea that will enter the human mind
We do not fight like this world; our weapons are not the same

We fight against the evils of this world calling on **Jesus'** name
We are not moved or shaken by the threats of the enemy
We have no fear because we know in whom we do believe
One thing we must remember our flesh is not our friend
Our spirit fights constantly against our flesh
We must not let it win
He has given us the whole armor to stand
It takes faith to fight and understand
The helmet of **salvation**, the breastplate of **righteousness**, the belt of **truth**
The gospel of **peace** to cover our feet, the shield of **faith** to believe, and the **Word of God** as our sword to bring us into one accord
Use your weapons of **praise, worship** and **prayer** to subdue the enemy under your feet
To fight in the spiritual realm the things you cannot see
He has given us power and authority to win
We claim the victory over satan and sin
This is a spiritual war.

Last Days

The last days are here
Signs are everywhere
Evil runs rampant through the land
Destroying all it can
Families and homes are being torn apart
So much hatred and anger inside men's hearts
Infidelity and impurity is accepted as the norm
Alternative lifestyle and homosexuality is taking us by storm
Society wants the whole world to conform
Parents leaving children unattended, abused and neglected
Forgetting and turning their backs on the God they have rejected
Mothers against daughters and fathers against sons
The bible clearly let us know the last days has begun
War and terror in our backyards and across the land
The world's minds and eyes have been blinded
They cannot understand
Their hearts are hard and callous and cannot feel
They cannot discern what is false or what is real
Living in despair and moral decay
Wanting the church to decree that sinning is okay
Heady and high minded wearing pride as a cover
Wanting approval to have more than one lover
Discrimination, injustice and prejudice still exist
Malice, jealousy and deceit is prevalent in our midst
Anger and bitterness is rooted so deep
With walls of resentment strong as cement

They can't even weep
Fear taking control of men's heart
Afraid to commitment to Christ, so they stay apart away from him
The outward appearance looks good to the public eye
But their private life knows you are living a lie
Trying hard to cover their "secret sins"
Instead of exposing the devil, so they can begin living free
Government looking, searching frantically for a solution
To end economic woes and world pollution
Hiding behind high positions, status and titles
Not realizing they have become damnable idols
Pretending to be spiritual with a form of godliness
In reality your carnality is preparing you for the abyss
God had a brilliant plan
How to save fallen man
He thought he would send himself
So he wrapped up in human flesh
He used the gift of love and grace
To rescue the entire human race
To make it out of the last days alive
In order to thrive and not just survive
You have to surrender to the One with the plan
The One who died for sinful man
Jesus Christ
He is the Way, the Truth and the Light
He is the only hope to survive the last of the last days.

The Remnant

There is a remnant who yet believe
That there is but one God, not two or three
God wrapped himself in humanity
As Jesus he came down to earth
Through Mary, a virgin birth
There is a remnant who believe that Jesus is the Messiah
The promised One, God's only begotten son
Lord, you allowed me to walk this path of life to see
There are so many who do not believe
They do not believe that Christ is real
Their eyes are blinded to the Word, Christ revealed
Sealed in their conscience
Deceived in their own mind
Seeking life's answers but unable to find
Not knowing that life without Christ is not really living
Today receive the abundant life Christ is giving
He will return for those who do believe
It is heaven or hell, which one will you receive?

Jesus is the Light

What is night
It is the absence of light
With you Lord, it is never
Night
You are the Light
Your word declares
Night and day are the same to you
You are light and
No darkness can dwell in your presence
Nor tarry in your sight
You are Holy
You were before the world begin
You are Sovereign and with you
There is no end
You still open eyes to see
You still unstop ears to hear
You are the Light of the world
You are which is, which was and is to come
Praise God for the Light!

House of Clay

One day this house of clay will be laid to rest
From all its labor and its test
Soon I will be in my heavenly home
Dancing and praising around God's throne
No more sadness, no more tears
No more heavy burdens to bear
Forever in the presence of the Almighty King
Where he reigns and he is Supreme
The angels bow and worship before him continuously
I will join with them at His feet
All my heartaches and pain will be no more
I will be in eternity with the one I adore
Death, hell and the grave cannot rule over me
Because my spirit will have complete authority
I am grateful for the comfort I find in my Savior's embrace
It is just by His amazing grace that I continued to run this race
Longing for the day when I will be at peace and see His face.

Deliver Me

Deliver me from
Me
Deliver me from
Self-righteousness
Selfishness
Deliver me at times when
I cannot see
At times I do not believe
Deliver me from the pride
That hides deep inside
Deliver me from judgment
Of other's wrong
Lest I forget how you suffered long
With me
Deliver me from the attitude
That I am so good
When I know there is but
One who is good and
Let me love as I should

Deliver me
Help me to be merciful
To show mercy so that
I may obtain mercy
Help me to be kind
Remove all the sin you find
Cleanse my heart and
Cleanse my hands
Open my eyes to understand
Your will and your way
Use me as a vessel
I pray
To reach the lost, the hurt
Outcast and confused
I just want to be used
Deliver me from me
The real me
Only you can see
Please Lord, deliver me!

Prayer Changes Things

I can't quit now
Nor will I give up
I may have to drink
From this bitter cup
But
I must fulfill the purpose
Designed by my pain
I must remember there is power
In your Holy name
So when I fall down on my knees
You pay attention to my every plea
When I pray, I believe Heaven moves
My God has promised I will not lose
He has prepared the heavenly host to fight
To defeat the devil and put him to flight
I must take my rightful place and with authority
Rebuke the enemy and he will flee
Bind up his plots, tricks and plans
God want us free, every child, woman and man.

He Knows

Weary soul, take your rest
Your heavenly Father knows best
He knows the way that you must go
He knows the highs and He knows the lows
He knows the valleys and the peaks
It is important His face to seek
He wants us to totally place our trust in Him
Not to be shaken by every whelm
He is our Father and He really does care
Nothing that concerns **you** catches Him unaware
Before the beginning He had a plan
How He would save fallen man
Many times we do not understand
We must be willing to put it **all** into His hands
The trials of life comes to make us strong
To build our muscles as we hold on
They come to teach us how to obey and submit
How to make Jesus your Lord and to Him commit
He knows.

Testimony

The greater the test
The greater the anointing
Without trouble or test
There would be no testimony
The greater the test
The greater the anointing
Lord I desire a fresh outpouring
Of your Spirit

The test is preparing me
For my future and destiny
Increase my faith
To believe
Help me to walk
Where you lead
I have a testimony because of the test
The crushing and pressure has brought out my best
I am a witness, He will bring you out
Only trust and do not doubt
Greater is He that is in us than he that is in the world.

I Can't Afford

I can't afford to be off focus
Wandering through life hocus pocus
I can't afford not to forgive
Knowing it's the only way I can live
I can't afford to be disobedient
With me He has been so lenient
I can't afford not to love
When I say I represent the One above
I can't afford not to be kind
He has showered blessings on all mankind
I can't afford not to live right
As He gives me wisdom and insight
I can't afford to waste time
I must be a good steward of what is not mine
I can't afford not to laugh
It may be the only moment left that I have
I can't afford not to take heed
Warning comes before destruction you see
I can't afford not to seek His face
To ask for mercy, forgiveness and grace
I can't afford not to pray
I need His guidance every day

I can't afford not to believe
I ask Him for faith as eyes to see
I can't afford distractions to get me off track
I resist the devil to keep him off my back
I can't afford negative reports to fill my thoughts
I mediate on His word as I ought
I can't afford not to follow His lead
It is the only way I will succeed
I can't afford to ask amiss
His blessing and promises I don't want to miss
I can't afford to miss His voice
I am glad I made Him my choice
I can't afford not to hear
He makes my pathway clear
I can't afford not to be thankful or
Grateful because He is faithful
I can't afford living without him
It is like hanging out on a shaky limb
I can't afford to be left behind
He is coming soon, just look at the signs.

There Will Be Glory

There will be glory after the pain
After the heartache and the shame
God's glory will be revealed
He will cause all wounds to heal
It was designed to be this way
He put in you what was needed to stay
He knew the integrity He built into you
He knew the path you must travel through
No it did not feel good to your flesh
But the flesh must die so He could rise
It pleased Him to choose you for this test
He knew it would only bring out your best
He knew the opposition would strengthen you
Although you really did not have a clue
He ordered this assignment to build your faith
This kind of faith is what it will take
To go into the next level of His anointing and grace
Fervent prayers and fasting as you seek His face

Deliverance will come when you hold fast and believe
He has already assured you the Victory
Stand strong and hold on
He knows the way you must go
It is not to kill you but for you to grow
He knows just how much you can bear
He has bottled up all your tears
You are precious in His sight
He wants you to rely on him for your light
There will be glory after all
Even though at times you may fall
Your weaknesses yes may be exposed
But it is not really what you suppose
God chastens those whom He love
With His grace and tender mercy from above
He wants to make sure you see His face in peace
He wants the inner turmoil to cease so you can live in liberty.

Good Morning

It is the dawn of a brand new day
Weeping is gone and joy is here to stay
Midnight has passed and there is
Eternal light at last
No more heartaches, no more pain
No more disappointments, no more shame
There shall be peace at last
For those who withstood the stormy past
Those who held on to the promise of rest
And for those who endured the fiery test
Good morning, joy is here
No more sickness, no more tears
Nor heavy burdens to bear
Just praise and worship to our King
He is the reason why we can sing
Good morning
All of God's promises are true
He told you He would see you through

The darkness and fear of midnight
He promised He would be your light
He promised it was all for your good
If you would trust Him like you should
He promised it was only for a season
To recognize Him as Lord was the reason
He promised at the times when you felt unsure
Trust in Him s your anchor will be sure
He promised that after the pouring rain
He would be the grace to sustain
He would relieve your pain
Because **all power** is in his name
He promised
You would definitely see the sun shine again
Good morning!